Imago Mundi

Michelle Mitchell-Foust

Elixir Press

Imago Mundi

Grateful acknowledgment is made to the editors and publishers of the following publications in which poems from this manuscript appear:

Colorado Review, "Model for Simberg's 'Wounded Angel'" and "Imago Mundi III"; *Denver Quarterly*, "Migraine Ghazal" and "Abacus of Birds for Eurydice"; *Elixir*, "Argument for the Ghost," "Hologram" (abridged), and "Three of Mary"; *The Nation*, "At the Green Cabaret"; *Perihelion,* "Us in the Dark Wandering Home,'" Eurydice at Mammoth Caves, 1983," and "Imago Mundi I."

Also by Michelle Mitchell-Foust, *Circassian Girl*, Elixir Press (2001).

Cover Art: *Seigfried's Difficult Way to Brunhilde*, 1991, Anselm Kiefer
               Photograph and lead in a glazed steel frame
               170 x 240 cm. (66 7/8 x 94 1/2 in.)
               Courtesy of Lia Rumma
Cover Design: Adrienne Sappa
Author Photo: Carole Patterson

ISBN: 1-932418-12-1

Elixir Press is a non-profit literary organization.

Elixir Press
P. O. Box 27029
Denver, CO 80227
www.elixirpress.com

Table of Contents

for Kevin

and for Karen and Carl Hume Mitchell

Migraine Ghazal

A child walking home has her first.
The noon hysteria of dandelions

moves to its home behind one eye.
Noon becomes a snow patch.

Noon anesthetizes her, loosening
her hold on the school book.

Then there are hundreds of flowers
in her head, all the same color,

blooming to escape the snow,
threatening to bloom repeatedly there.

I.

Model for Simberg's "Wounded Angel"

The exiles are passing by
with their brushes and
cleaning solutions.

They remind her
that everything she does *from now on*
is of her own volition,

especially her listening at the door
for a swish of hair, for *something*
around the various echoes

that are the mainstay
of the cool darkness
of the empty schoolroom.

A name whistles inside her,
a molecule, little flesh chime,
the tiny distress call

of a single, white Barbie shoe
turned on its side
in the drive.

An airsickness band falls
from her purse, gray,
lint-covered. It takes

its time falling.
This is as true for angels
as it is for women:

outer space plays hell
with their bone density,
but this is the way the sky

works, marbled like a searchlight
shining through the end
of a drum,

shallowing the cartilage
that holds together wings.
Then comes the night,

lax, skewered on two poles
like an animal on a spit,
its good smell in her throat,

and the boys who carry
the weight of night
don't breathe heavy.

One pours ether
on a hot shovel
to ease its passage

for the whole world.
She knows this
because she's written

the caption for this moment
herself, a million times.
"I'm the molecule's chill fleet.
I am the flame, I know."

At the Green Cabaret

after Rimbaud

I braved the frozen road for this:
bread and butter, a coke, the animal
world of this booth and the couple
at the next table, browsing

a vacation brochure entitled
Endless Vacation, and a girl
pushing a woman in a wheelchair
to the counter, where she pulled

off her hood and ran, absent-
mindedly, a hand through her
purpled hair, as if it weren't
purple, as though crayola purple

were the most natural color
in the world for hair, and
she bought three shortbread
cookies, and wheeled her friend out,

her hair a cotton-candy blaze
in the winter sun of the restaurant
foyer, and her cheeks
burning on the cold.

Abacus of Birds for Eurydice

I hear a saw first,
and then nothing for a long time,
then the saw again, and all day
I don't know whether to miss it
when it's gone,
or wish it away entirely.

Should I hate the harvest?

Mostly, I've had that dream again,
the one where we are reading
a play, and I'm to read
the fairy part,
but someone else
starts where I should,

and I look up,
as if to say
I am the woman, then?

*

It was nice of you
to send those pictures,
though I couldn't bring myself
to look at them.
I've had a woman here
tell me what they are.

She says, in one, the sky
is covered. The bee hives
disappear around a tree,
with only a few of the bees
showing.

They look quiet,
from almost any distance.

Without you, I replace
the sounds of the bees
in your photograph for birds

swarming, and the birds
for leaves, and your hand
on my hair for the sound
of my waking from a nap.

Hell has a sound like the hive's
moving quiet. It must,
for its hands

are places *without end,
and no place
where nothing happens.*

Inside them,
a hundred lovers sound
like one deceptive one
throwing her voice.

*

My first night, I slept
outside the humming room.
I had to, because in my confusion,
I kissed the man at the door.

You wouldn't believe
how slowly the light
from where you are
moves out of him.

Three of Mary

New Orleans, 2002

We almost don't find the ex-votos
    at St. Roch's.

The city is a glass child half-sunk
in water. The water is fountain water.
The fountain is in the courtyard
behind the green shutters.

At her spleen (away from the mouth
of the Mississippi, black Santas hanging
on the houses) is a cemetery window
in a cathedral. And through the window

is a room of healing, the odd relics
locked away from the children
who play around the graves
that border the cathedral.

The sill is covered with ashes.
Our elbows are covered with ashes,
our hands dusty from the glass,
and the children somewhere behind us

scream in the cold sun.
We see through the window
of the healing room: the sun hitting
the bottom of a foot, a foot hanging

broken at the heel, a stone face, a hand
hanging, an ear, the shadows of the window bars
hitting two stone hands cupping two stone birds
and thirty-three carved **thanks**

around Mary's head that hangs
upside down on a hook.
We ask that our colds be cured.
And the sun misses the crumbled plaster

in a statue child's hair as the clock
strikes three, a ball of something sewn
tight with brown thread, several of them,
wool I mistake for dog toys lying doggedly

at Mary's feet, and at the feet of some other saint,
and my husband says, no, not dog toys.
Didn't they insulate their plaster casts
with wool?

Rap music from somewhere, we keep looking.
He keeps taking pictures through the window.
I know the no-headed angel with the worm
on her sleeve is content. Her arms folded

just so in her lap. Under the saints and over
the rusted flowers she crosses her bare feet
at the ankle: rose, roser, rosest,
brown like old blood.

The husks of locusts at Mary's feet
remind us of the plague these offerings survived,
whose wearers lived to leave them here,
whose mouths left with their ghosts.

II.   You may grow more desperate.
           I may read about you.

A bronze hinge drops from nowhere
into a room where I tell the story
of the murderer's house:

The walk in the cold
to the murderer's house,
the attic where she murdered.

The tangle of her hair.
The stones falling out of the tomb.
The ghost of the girl falling from the roof.

What is the state of privacy in the afterlife?
The dead on Governor Nichols St.
have none, particularly

the girl-now-ghost
in the shape of the box
she was cut to fit inside.

I hate to admit
I was watching
for the house all the time,

all over the quarter,
as if it might come up to me
from behind, even in broad daylight

and whisper: "You may grow
more desperate. I may
read about you."

My husband takes its picture
at night, and he takes its picture
again in the morning. Either way,

I feel the same leap
when I see a jean jacket
and backpack

hanging in a tree
along a busy street.
A girl's backpack,

and her jacket, small and black,
ominous in the evening.
No sign of the girl—

an absence as terrifying
as a bronze hinge
falling from nowhere

into a room,
the ringing on the carpet
that stops me from finishing the story

of the walk in the cold.
No one will touch the hinge
at first, and when an older

Chinese woman brings it up to me,
heavy, not a scratch on it,
I won't take it home.

She believes it belongs to me now.
But no one can say where it
fell from. No one can guess

its origin, so no one wants
to touch it, which seems the opposite
of faith, except the truth is

we all become children again
in its presence. The murderer
flinging us into the cold,

the old bottles flashing a red water
in the window of the pharmacy
in honor of Christmas,

the transplanted convent
with nothing more fancy
than a streetlight.

*Who **knows** who*
started the fire
that brought the dead girl to light.

In the classroom,
I hold up my *grie grie*—
my plantation key, my souvenir

of the world behind the world,
the bronze hinge's fall
still ringing in our ears,

and someone says the word "manacle"
from the back of the room, and I think
door, no, **door,**

and I feel a dark shadow pass.
I know the muse for this
is a child.

III.   The smell of vetiver powder, bundles of vetiver,
       and pictures of vetiver growing.

God the child, or the child of the voodoo priestess, or the
murderer's child, the girl she murdered. The smell of vetiver
grass brings back the mob in the painting of New Orleans. In a
room where I tutor a boy, above our heads the whole time
without my knowing, a beige and brown painting of the
outskirts, the dark water of the foreground, a huge old house
back away from us, and floating crowded together in the upper
right-hand corner, a beige mob, the faces of men around a picnic
table, a few women in the back, practically mouthless. No sign of
Mary. The boy says the painting is about the sadness of the
paintees. He eats the gaudy King Cake his relatives sent from the
very setting of the painting above our heads while I look for the
words in the liquids category: solutes, solvents, salts. They
explain the weary head of water. The snowy egret lifts in the
bayou. The pink clothespin on a string in the bearded tree waits
on one of the older heavier alligators.

IV.   At a famous wedding supper, the ghost of a child nestling
      in the bride's lap.

I can't find the passage in Nabokov's memoir about privacy in
the afterlife.

He says his mother liked looking for mushrooms, the way my
own father did when I was a child.

He confesses a love for ski lifts and for a dog who smells either like
saltines or brown sugar when he's fresh from bed in the morning.

He's invented colors for the alphabet: *a has the tint of weathered
wood, b has the tone called burnt sienna by painters, c has the curious
mixture of azure and mother-of-pearl*, the color we always see Mary
wearing.

We find cough drops on Governor Nichols St. in the antique
pharmacy, and Nabokov has been here all along: the man who
loved ski lifts, whose wife drove him around and around America
in a car.

Like the school pictures girls tape on their dressers, a black
and white movie photograph of Humbert Humbert and Lolita
stares at me, snug in the soda fountain mirror.

There's an ice cream Sunday in front of Lolita, on the very counter
where I'm resting my arms. I'm in her seat. I'm leaning over to
see the picture of her better.

A bee, thawed by the pharmacy, rises and bumps against the ceiling.
A Russian winter is far away, a centaur looking back over its
shoulder in the woods.

I leave Mary's face behind in a taxi on Royal St., Royal and Governor Nichols, where the Haunted House is, where a woman threw a child off the roof.

It is raining. Mary's face is painted in black ink on a ripe tomato red bag I got for Christmas, and inside the bag is one pair of warm socks and my umbrella from New York. Look, I think she's getting away.

V.   No one remembers the face of Marie Laveau.

That reach for the stingray that wet her sleeve—a slick
memory asking to be added to—a small plane flying low over
the river outside the window, low in a straight line. Marie the poet
admires my scarf in the cold foyer of the Methodist church.
Two of six lamps swinging, the headstone clocks, the
headstone switches. My husband taking my picture again and
again, staying warm in the cold foyer with wine and pictures.
I can't stop laughing. There are two Christmas trees at the
altar, one on each side, and I can't remember any decorated
trees at my old Methodist church.

We take the ferry to Algiers, the many churches in Algiers.
The shells instead of gravel on the streets of that small town
across the Mississippi, where they keep the parade floats and giant
albino flamingos blessedly out of range of the unbearable pipe
organ on the riverboat. In Algiers, the face of the voodoo priestess
is somewhere between man and woman, two of six lamps swinging
in her sanctuary, three of one hundred Xs visible in the distance.

Someone put Marie Laveau in a poem and her sleeve is still wet
from her reach into the pool to touch an eel, or is it a stingray? (I
forget.) She is wonderful. She isn't thinking of herself as being in
a poem. She is only being tired in the aquarium, where she maybe
waits for a man. She isn't being in a poem. She is the poem. She
keeps her secret, and gives it away at the same time, the exchange
between mouth and eyes, eyes and mouth, never both lit up at
the same time. The flip side of her image is a mirror, not
necessarily the wet sleeve from the back and the back of her
skirt to the floor.

In the poem she gets blamed for a fire, and she smiles and says, *leave a cunning stone on my grave if you think that's true*. She wrings out her sleeve against the aquarium wall. The marble wall is wet from it, invisibly. By her hip, in a back-lit mermaid's purse, a tiny shark embryo squirms, no, two squirm in the box of water, and in another box of water there is a little dragon just out of reach of her skirt. The dragon with leaves for hands: a sea animal to remember her by, another woman whose face escapes history. On her bathroom floor in the poem, wings from an infestation. The soldiers died against her broom, but no getting rid of the wings; like sand, like war, they won't leave.

Outside her house the Christmas tree in the courtyard's all hung with beads, all year round. No sign of Mary at first, but the son of man is a doll under the cheery tree, whose arms and legs stay in the crawling position, though he's on his back, without any clothes on, arms and legs bent motionless in the air, in an oddly happy scene. This could be a scapular medal next (only not soft, not worn under the clothes, with Mary slid inside the warm window fogged from a woman's skin): A picture of Mary in a tiny silver frame hangs from a dog-tag on the tree. A black pearl dangles from the frame: She rides a horse. She is barefooted standing on the horse in her dark skirt and blouse, hair and mane sailing, hair wet at her neck. She is smiling with her arms straight out at her sides.

On the back of the photo in a female hand: ***m*** *is a fold of your pink flannel … I thought I saw you blink … I saw you at prayer … I thought I saw you waiting for your turn*. And Mary's silver belt shines in the picture. Her spirit stays in the small pig's tail at the petting zoo, small black tail straight as a dog's because it's too young to curl. It never stops wagging.

VI.   When there's no difference between the ghost
       of a house and the person who visits the ghost.

       (at the St. Vincent's Guest House)

There is a boy stopped spider-like along
the outside of the building across the street.
He's stopped at one massive gray corner,
the top of his head facing us, a green stone boy
instead of a gargoyle, and the light changes,
and he moves again, in full view of our room,
in the old infant-asylum-turned-hotel.

We didn't know what he was at first.
How far away that made him from us.
Now we know. Now we hear the knocking ghost
in our room. In the closet, under the sink.
The muse for this is a child whose voice
has gone, but his ghost stays in the white
ceiling fan, and in the pipes.

Mary stands to the side of the infant asylum.
She might be made of snow. She's glacially white.
Her huge stone aura keeps her from looking
over her shoulder, so the asylum has a boy
on one side, and Mary on the other. At night
they are only stone that looks like snow.
At night they are dreaming and give no answer.

Once, the snow on a fence post
scared me to death. I was in the mountains.
I was sure I was seeing Mary outside
the cottage window, the calm mother
before Easter, her veil white-blue under
the streetlight, and the blizzard
I hadn't seen for years coming down

around her. She was only feet
from the glass, and without a halo.
All her light came from behind her skin.
My grandfather was working in a factory
when Mary appeared at the foot of his bed,
no snow on the bedpost, and he still
follows her call.

I am not imagining Mary outside
the infant asylum. I am not imagining her
inside. One of the women who cooks here
has one leg shorter than the other,
pool in the courtyard covered with leaves,
a real Christmas tree on the stairs,
and smile self-conscious of teeth.

How can I not imagine this woman
was here when the asylum children
came into the world? With their squalls.
Their ghosts. She serves grits to the tourists,
most who've never eaten grits before,
most who'll return home from their holiday
to find their lives make little sense for awhile.

I want to give them my father's
grits recipe after she leaves the plate.
Not salt, but syrup over the butter,
the leftovers palmed and squared
and fried, and syrup poured over them.
I want to give them my grandfather's recipe
for knowing Mary when you see her.

II.

Us in the Dark Wandering Home

Falcarragh, Ireland

For Kevin and Pam

I found the Aristotle paraphrases
of Albertus Magnus, and the milky way
was certainly full of stars. I couldn't stop
reading the revision of Magnus saying the lunar
rainbow appeared to him twice in one year,
not the once-in-fifty-years of Aristotle.
I have only seen the lunar rainbow once in a lifetime,
over the high bog of an ancient gravesite
lit by a ringed moon. The whole thing
with a small rain.

It was midnight and the arch was black
and every color, and the new burros and sheep
made such a racket instead of sleeping
that we knew we were seeing something profound
among the sock puppet headstones
in the deep August light, us wondering whether
the souls of the layers of the dead beneath us warmed
to the rain under the phenomenon,
us in the dark wandering home.

Pam at the Rock of Forgetting

I.

We don't stay by the water long at dusk
on the way to the encephalitis scare and
all the broken quiet when two blue herons

bang against the water and mad-dash up again
like teens. They mirror the doves landing
for a second on the tin lining of the star deck.

An average light grazes the windows, average
for the orange-glorious evenings of fall, and gravity
breathes the Greek word for *ribbon* into our muscles,

the clouds for this last moment of light looking pulled up
by the roots. We find two starfish, one in this world,
and one in another, and we throw both back into the sea.

II.

I know the priest has begun to leave tomatoes
at the door in Stonington,
the only speck of blood that makes our day.

I find a meteorite in a gallery and think
the world might be destroyed by this, heavier
than it looks, falling five thousand miles an hour

during this last shower. A young woman selling
pricey lingerie tells me she has seen the insides
of a meteorite, so marvelous inside that she asked a guard

for the artist's name at the exhibition. She was sure
the split star had been carved, so meticulous
the labyrinth was, and she begs me to break mine in half.

You have to break it, she whispers, and she draws the squares
of lines on a perfume sample to show me, breathing audibly
as she draws. The semi-precious stones are the ones

to watch out for, our invisible host said once,
and in his copy of Ponge's *The Young Girl*, he's underlined
throat. He's written, *gage=blossoms*.

What can you measure with a blossom but love?
Now, they're saying, with the new software,
we can measure everything on earth by the flower's

inner spiral——a new sign of the host——
even the eerie leap of the razor from my hand,
even the miraculous distance between my hand and your face.

III.

Days I have been in the secret room
I leave a single shell among
the quartzes. Its insides have the sound

of the low whistle of wind through Coney Island's
metal rides, the live swans strolling
the roadside water, perfect as an arcade game.

I leave a chocolate on the old host's headstone
and head for school, where a woman
rushes up behind me, both of us

entering a gallery of student paintings,
and whispering *Go left. Go left.* so that
both of us expect to follow her voice,

and upon entering the hall, she looks around
and turns to me, her sweater pink and glowing,
and says, *He lied to me. He lied to me.*

She runs for the corner to the other hall,
and disappears, all the while hoping
that she is wrong about him.

IV.

In the commons, a maintenance man stops
his small truck to cut a woman's ring off,
and the wire cutters bird over her as she laughs.

It's over, I guess. It's outside the college cafeteria
that smells like a circus midway, a burned sugar
hovering over the metal umbrellas, the convicts in lime green

folding the carnival rides from some two-day fair
in on themselves, just outside the school grounds.
I am wearing the souvenir shell around my neck——

a real shell once dipped in silver somewhere
behind the lighthouse all hung with bones.
I'm so homesick for the strange place

that I might as well be putting together an oscillating fan
a beloved has sent, not knowing what I needed.
Any time of day, I can turn the silver-covered shell over,

and a little water pours down my dress.
No matter when the bath was, no matter
that I've already accidentally turned the shell

over in the car, running a hand along my collar
in traffic, or tipped it over by writing on the board.
Watch Hill's just an arm-length away,

the juxtaposition of outrigger and of little boy
who skips as a bird lifts from the playground.
The genuine cross of hand and bird make it seem as though

the boy is throwing the crow up into the burning clouds
with his own hands, lovely to distraction,
like a table of shells for sale in the sun.

Argument for the Ghost

I.

The crow and gamble of my life
suggests, at the point

when memory catches
the light, a crow who fumbles

through the over-turned
orange grove, as though

he hadn't a wing to his name,
is slang for the word *enthusiastic*

as much as the other birds
singing in the dark.

II.

How a ghost catches
on a room: I saw a woman
at her picnic, her weekday
picnic, the back of her legs
as pale as her enormous dress.

The way a ghost catches
on a room is the way her
enormous dress catches
on her hip at the picnic table,
betrays her body under there
under the dress.

I have forgotten the name
of the yellow flower
I smell in the room
I believe she haunts:
the flower the ghost loves,
the smell she comes
in the shape of.

She isn't a terror,
but I've asked her
not to show herself to me
while I'm awake.

*

One terror and then another:
that merely
by carrying it
in an open palm,
a palm all but flat,
you've ruined the blue egg
for its mother.

*

She's only shown the white
sheath of herself to my husband
in the middle of the night,
and he refuses to remember her.

III.

okay   At night, everyone in the room
                   knew she was there.

alright   Below the staircase she'd fallen
                   over the side

                   as though stairs
                   were ships.

*

                   She's visible, under all
                   their convincing,

                   for only a second.

we weren't
breathing   long hair, blood on her,
                   on the floor.

                   She disappeared again,
                   but everyone behind me

                   in the room, invisible
                   as she was,

                   knew she was still there.

*

They keep
saying it   I put my hand out into space
                and feel her gasp

                the gasp of the knifethrower's
                new target.

IV.

Humerulus, alula, bullula, mentum,
rostellum, sagum, surculus, the
genitalia of blue.

My husband (the skeptic!)
waves a smoking bundle
of white sage around the house
to ward her off. I'm not sure
I want him to. The bundle's
the color of frost,

the half-hidden weather
of webs inside webs
that look like stars.

Finally, she's sleeping
enough to dream.

At El Campo Santo (The Holy Fields)

Scalloped crosses so white against the black ground,
and bordering the graves the picket fences
and tourists in the sun with their arms around
themselves or with their hands behind them
saying they don't mean to intrude on the powers
in this place. *One and Twenty years I have seen,*
it says, *the fields planted with flowers.*
I was young, I called to god. Don't cry for me.
The crosses hang with cranberries for Christmas
with crow-bitten popcorn around the cross limbs
and with many a single rose made of twisted dusty
corn husk over where the body is, lovely, with a girl with
hiccups taking away some of the dead silence (like sails
on the far sea) and the light, soon pink, getting carried away.

III.

Eurydice at *Mammoth Caves,* 1983

Prologue

"Eurydice at Mammoth Caves, 1983" and "Hologram" are two chapters of the same poem, both set at Mammoth Caves. In the first, the Eurydice of Greek mythology finds herself in the caves after the fatal bite to her foot on her wedding day. (Some members of her wedding actually show up in the caves.) She's traveled from Sadorus, Illinois, her hometown in the poem, to Mammoth Caves.

In the second chapter of the poem, the story of Harlequin, Columbine, and Pierrot, of Italian myth, surrounds Eurydice's wanderings through the caves. For ages, children all over Europe learn in the old stories that Harlequin was a wonderful dancer, that he ran away from home to dance on the streets of the city near his home. But he didn't want to be recognized, or be forced to return home, so he wore a mask and never took it off.

Harlequin met a marvelous fiddler on his travels, and he danced to the fiddler's songs. Together they entered the city, and there, Harlequin met the doctor's daughter Columbine, and she loved watching him dance, but she was already promised to a sea captain, and her father (with her father's assistant Pierrot) watched her like a hawk. Tricking the doctor with the order of phony house-calls, the fiddler (with Pierrot's help) made sure that Harlequin and Columbine had time together, though she danced on the balcony, and Harlequin danced below her, still wearing the mask. Eventually, Harlequin and Columbine ran off together.

"Hologram" is set several years down the road from the narrative of the children's tale. Columbine's affections for the trickster Harlequin have cooled, and Harlequin, still wearing his mask, wanders the crawlspace of these mythic mammoth caves.

The child chorus of the poem encourages Eurydice to find Harlequin in the caves. They are destined to become confidantes.

The "Lost" Maps in the poem are inspired by the work of Irish artist Kathy Prendergast from *The End and the Beginning*. The old swimming pool images of Pierrot's final soliloquy were inspired by Anselm Kiefer's work *I Hold All Indias in My Hand*.

Futhermore

The tallest man in the world was Robert Wadlow. He died of an infection in his foot.
"Elephant" is another word for Inn.
Pogonophora riftia is a giant tube worm with red feathers. It was discovered ten years ago by marine biologists.

Stage Directions

What is lit. One thing at a time. In the cave. In the cave Harlequin is always juggling, sometimes a coin. Columbine is smoking.

Eurydice at *Mammoth Caves*, 1983

> "She was there, limping a little
> From her late wound, with the new shades of Hell.
> And Orpheus received her, but one term
> Was set: he must not, till he passed Avernus,
> Turn back his gaze, or the gift would be in vain."
> The Metamorphosis of Ovid

> "Concerning love, I know a conjugation…."
> John Nash

I.

They take our picture
before we go down

into the cave,
in case one of us

goes missing,
thirty or forty of us,

some of us too pale
in our summer clothes.

(I think I
closed my eyes,)

managed to miss
the white doors (doves?)

flying from a truck
onto the road.

I lose track of the truck
and the sirens

but not the fire,
a bird buzzing my cheek.

I look in a windshield
to make sure it's gone

and see how black the bird
must have been against my hair.

II.

The tour bus idles on the gravel,
a child cries because

she left her money at home,
I'll tell you what the dead want:

not to go missing from the picture
they take.

They are the slow eye.
They are not missing, I tell them.

They put a rock down
to stop the photograph of us

from whipping around
like a bird in the house.

They sign the back
H   E   Double Toothpicks.

III.

 A fan blows all the other group photos
of forty-or-so people who might go missing

in the split second of the camera flash.
In the split second of seeing an 8

or a 3 in the camera flash, I turn
the number on its side, and it's

eternity, or half eternity.
It's forever,

a dismembered newspaper
flapping in the teeth of a palm.

IV.

I go missing. Sunburned
red geranium smell, strong

even as I turn a number
on its side, and it's forever.

The man I love consults the picture
all night. There I am,

a likeness
to numbers

on the wall by now.
In the copy.

*

They have an easel
up against the mountains

with an oil
of the hill

exactly as it looks,
except for a cloud

not in the actual sky
that breaks and spreads

like a sunrise,
no painter anywhere,

just the oil
left with the weather.

V.

The seals sound like birds.
The birds sounds like seals.

The children with their backs
to the headstones

draw the new house
across the street,

the frantic creaking door
of a great heron,

wings beating prehistoric
over the roof.

Maybe they will draw me
from memory.

VI.

The egrets fan from one tree
to the other above a picnic.

Their voices are under-water voices,
or mouths coming up for air.

A crow screams at its reflection
in the gift shop window.

That bird hates gifts,
a child says, watching it scream.

VII.

They have colored lights
around the stalactites

and cartoon characters
placed here and there

around the stalagmites,
cooling the blow

of the sublime,
and they have potted roses,

beautiful in spite of
the rust, and a souvenir map

wrapped around
a pencil full of small stones.

Illegible. You can have one
for a song.

VIII.

Their map has terra-incognita
spaces

the old mapmakers called
sleeping beauties,

where the line stops
and starts again,

no accounting
for the birds inside,

for the umbrella
over the sea.

My imagination
to my desire,

makes something
inside the trees.

My foot hurts
inside my shoe,

but not enough hurt
to stop walking.

A song
is every sleeping beauty.

IX.

They have a throat singer
whose one voice

sounds like a number of them.
Spooky undertow

inside one mouth,
he sings the sounds

of the air near water.
I try my hand

and send up a cloud of gulls.
He sings so strong

we feel the vibrations.
Sometimes we don't know

the vibrations are there
until they stop.

The jaw at rest.
Our jaw at rest.

Our role models
invisible.

For instance
the ghost

of the tallest man
in the world

who limps as I do,
whose foot killed him, too.

In the Masonic temple
they know him

because in life,
just like now,

he has to walk sideways
up the stairs.

X.

They have Jacob's Ladder
which our tour guide keeps saying is

bottomless. I believe him.
I've never come to the end.

Therefore they have *pogonophora riftia*,
the mammoth worm with the red plume

and black smoker ocean vents
that feed the fish

who don't feed on light.
Everything is red around the lower rungs.

My mother grew something
in a clear bowl (the world, I think),

nothing to do with leaves,
cave texture fingering up the insides

of the bowl, and laundry soap graininess,
interplanetary in pink and blue,

and there was a smell
back in the terrarium craze,

and quilts with crop circles
sewn onto them, and a goat

side-stepping
a water dish.

A gift like a cave should always
over-run the border.

XI.

They have the unfinished paintings
of Thalia Lincoln,

the half colored-in
birds of paradise.

They have a blonde child on a gray
heating and cooling unit

with a pink bucket on her head,
two white balls, one larger

at her feet. They have blue stars
on them, and behind the balls

sits a real white rabbit
with huge red markings.

The rabbit seems larger than the girl.
Large for its kind

as she is small
for hers.

XII.

In her Lavender "Mammoth Caves"
T-shirt, with little white footprints

running up to her right shoulder,
she sings.

If you look long enough at a word,
you can see it moving.

A word is never at rest.
The words on a girl's chest

move with her song.
She reminds us of a thousand years.

The small blonde
solitary reaper.

XIII.

They have a guide, a teen,
who says, *Sad heaven,*

enter me
before I kill again,

and several women
from the group photograph

who frown and laugh
and dig around inside their purses.

They no longer have to
think about

the two sounds
coming from the world's

shells. Maybe
they never have.

They have a petting zoo
with a pig's tail wagging,

and a tent away,
the yoga sellers

who will rub your shoulders
for five dollars.

XIV.

In the split second
of seeing an eight or a three,

the women know their young guide
complements their sulky daughters

who were made to leave
a boyfriend at home,

who covet a green kleenex
full of shells,

and a tiny (plush)
state fair extra-terrestrial.

XV.

Every sulky daughter covets
a typographical theme-park

portrait, thousands of numbers
instead of a face

when she looks up close,
eights or threes turning on their sides.

Funny to think
I'm one of those,

scrolling the concrete poem,
the thousands of numbers

that are Orpheus' head,
in my hands.

*

A child tries
to take back a spell:

Lemniscate. Lemniscate,
a scab of symbols.

(to the tune
"boil, boil").

She grieves because she tried
to show how another child

let his helium balloon go,
chimp face on the red balloon.

She let hers go *like this*
to show the boy next door,

both of them
looking up,

her hand still up
in the white sky

widening between her hand
and the white string,

her thinking
that her demonstration

is just that,
a specter balloon flying away.

She can keep her balloon
and let it go

like a secret,
like a number,

to show him
how people lost theirs.

The man I love
maybe thought

the same way
when I went missing,

a leopard in his mouth.
A special boat

getting away,
his yells are mine.

XVI.

They have a barn
a few miles up the road

with a black roof
that reads in white block

"Mammoth Caves (arrow
pointing left)".

They have
the ghost

of the world's
tallest man

walking sideways
up the stairs.

XVII.

To call the birds,
a single register is necessary.

I knew I wouldn't
be able to fly.

I wasn't
of a flight culture,

but I wanted
bird song

at my wedding.
We were going to throw doves

instead of rice
because bird song

is why you should stay
on earth, and why

you should not.

XVIII.

They have an Irish
famine painting here

of an Eagle's nest
where rests

a human leg.
In real life

the Donegal people
burned the leg.

They have no painting
of the burning.

XIX.

Soaked sheep's wool
caught on the gravel path

of the ancient ring
of cemetery.

Mary anchored
in a fishbowl there,

the grainy texture
of a headstone

enlarged by the water.
I mistook her for a mermaid.

Down the hill
the townspeople have filled

the tiny museum
with their own wedding dresses.

XX.

I have this life
soaked and strewn

as sheep's wool
around the cemetery gravel,

Mary suspended in water
like a goldfish

swimming
over someone's grave.

On my wedding day
my robe opened

when I opened
the curtains,

and I forgot
my relationship to the world,

and I (quick) hid my breasts
from the mountain.

No one expects my wedding party
in the curve of this cave

though people are always
getting married here.

Two ring bearers
enter the gift shop at a run,

their faces bracing
with the changing temperature

of the air.
In the split second

of seeing an eight or a three,
one ring-bearer

whose ribbon separated,
who has her little bracelet

on one plump hand
on her father's leg,

raises her eyebrows
instead of smiling into the camera.

The breath of the flowers
steams the glass.

Hologram

A Maschera

> *We tire of thinking and even of acting.*
> *We never tire of loving.*
> Auguste Compte

I.

(Child Chorus)

And something died
reaching back toward America,
hand out solid,
wet. Harlequin could never
end like this.

Here is where he began,
beside the manhole
in his inflated hat.

Letters on the manhole
spell out M A M M O

T H C A V E S.
The eyes behind the
ladder stones were
thousands of black,

and as with all manholes,
the rainy streets, the neon
red reflections.

<He steps over the arrow.
Leans against the image
of the MISSING GIRL.>

What a surprise
to hit dry earth.
What a surprise
the missing child had a ripped
tidbit from *Mlle. de Moulins*,

the gentle description
of a soap bubble pipe
like a nimbus
around her head,

and constellations, Virgo
and Leo, in color under the passage.
Death had cleaned the path
of water.

Viewmaster says: truck stop, empty road, oven, empty diner
booth, man's eye, hawk.

Note to self: (Harlequin): in the crawlspace, like a spelunker. He
edges toward the dark corner:

Dear Columbine:

> *You drove me to my prescription,*
> *so that I would know,*
> *every time, where to go,*
> *and then you took me*
> *to eat at the chicken restaurant,*
> *crowded with people*
> *too tired to lift a spatula*
> *in the early autumn dusk.*
> *The sun was going down*
> *on all of us. Columbine, we live*
> *in a world of counting.*

> *Harlequin*

II.   On a large movie screen in the caves. Like an old black and white movie.

(Columbine to Pierot): Looking at Two Portraits Side by Side.

It's just the color of her hair
makes her look pale.

And the ice pack.
That's how you know Eurydice.

You can't tell
from the picture

if she's alive
or dead.

When she orders a coffee
the cash register screen comes up

the figure in hiding,
instead of the price.

*

(Columbine, wistfully)

I can't save her
from the hand

reaching into
the picture of her.

It comes from the
typographical portrait

next to hers.
Seemingly,

the hand's
made of numbers.

We live
in a world of counting.

*

INT. MAMMOTH CAVES gift shop snack bar

Columbine changes the subject, patting her diamond quilt
souvenir. The camera moves of its own accord. Like accidental
photography. Sometimes a chin. Sometimes a whole face.

(Columbine)

What did father say when I left?

(Pierrot)

Dov, honey, here's the paper

(Columbine)

Newspapers make me crazy.
Just tell me what it says.

(Pierrot reads)

Polio didn't understand
what the sniper said
the first time.
They want him to call
them back. (Pierrot guffaws)

(Columbine)

Polio?

(Pierrot)

Or was it police? Typo.
The note was in heart-
broken English.
All my notes are in
heart-broken English.

      Did I tell you I was sitting
      next to a couple of beautiful
      Christian women in the Pizza place?
      The tiniest little neon sign
      reflected into the television
      and it covered one eye
      of the star anchor.

(Columbine)

You never said what father's doing.

(Pierrot)

He was moving "on all fives"
when you left.

Now he's declared the ocean a monster
who eats shells for candy.

(Columbine)

How do you know?

(Pierrot)

Postcard says as much.
He keeps writing that dreadful story

of a lunatic full of needles. He keeps
defining the word "autopsy" ….

(Child Chorus)

Ah. "To See for Oneself."

(Pierrot, changing the subject)

There is growing concern
for the ellipse.

Shall we
go back to Malmaison?

Witness whatever crawls out
of the exhibition?

I hear
all the women at the salons

and brothels in Rome are dressing
like marionettes at a children's theatre….

If not all the way back, maybe
just back to the Elephant.

*

(Child Chorus)

Pierrot wears no mask
though when you look at him
it's as though you are looking
into a windshield, and all you
see is the white sky over your
shoulder, and the tree
branches sprawling over
the glassy slope. You can just
make him out at dusk
behind the white sky.
He is everything beautiful
in the end of things.
He loves movies
with certain weathers,
snow, for instance.
He loves movies
with snow.

Viewmaster says: roofs of ranch style houses in every dull color.

Note to Self (Harlequin): in the crawlspace,

(*Note to Self* because even air
gets to the words before she does.):

Dear Columbine:

> *I've been thinking you were*
> *the largest shell I ever searched for,*
> *the ravishing slipping out of me*
> *like air, but you were*
> *a row of white houses,*
> *a dry lake someone*
> *was shouting about. You were*
> *the one shouting, violence*
> *the long name of a flower*
> *on your tongue. You were everyone*
> *in the dream.*

> *Harlequin*

III.

(Child Chorus)

Who knows the story
of the man who came to the woman

disguised as a key
grown beneath her skin?

The flesh grown over
the key in one night.

Her pale forearm
as mask,

he moved a little
when she moved,

hurt sometimes,
and broke the skin once

in her sleep several nights
down the road.

Lost
inside the covers,

she followed her own blood
to him.

But she was angry.
It was the last straw.

You are no bigger
than your voice

over the manhole,
Columbine said.

You are
smaller than your voice.

*

They were beings in excess of a lifetime.
One had only to insert the name of god,
and out they came from the telephone line,

apport, out of thin air, the warm breath
on one's face from his own mask. Harlequin
left death without his heart,

(saw Columbine *coming with it toward the ark*).

He's the thought that haunts the word,
his disguise, the Circassian Girl.
What could create this polygonal but a fly

lighting and lighting on the cave walls?
Why else have a ladder in every room?
The tyrant is heartbreak.

*

(Eurydice, wandering the old cave hospital and finding a child)

"Someone mistook me
for Columbine,

the red lipstick
mottled with sand.

Isn't she invisible?
Isn't her lover

in the crawlspace?
And isn't he invisible?"

(The child only stares
in disbelief. She speaks.)

"You must be she.
I can see your death

in your face, your gift
from Pierrot;

(he is already dead;
you can win against him)

look at the rainy red reflection
of yourself on the floor."

*

Viewmaster says of the Wedding Day:

An arm,
Bright sun,

Grass,
Unravelled cassette

In the sun,
Like tinsel,

Note to self (Harlequin): in the crawlspace:

Dear Columbine:

> *The snow surprised me, a soundless*
> *angel that lies*
> *unmade on the ground,*
> *its body blameless as the sky-*
> *colored pictures above the bed.*
> *And it's late. The canary sings sadly*
> *and incessantly behind me, a thread*
> *of you somewhere in his mad*
> *carefulness. There's the half-hearted snowball*
> *you made to throw at me*
> *near my heart, near the single, unlit hall*
> *light in this house. And I see*
> *I cannot see your face*
> *in much detail, only the garden*
> *I'll lie down in, in place*
> *of dying, and the harmless*
> *chairs, the perfect sheets.*
> *There are as many deaths as kinds of sleep.*

> *Harlequin*

IV.

(Child Chorus)

Edu-tainment, sprawl
the term. Harlequin, Columbine, Pierrot.

They left the group as a tree,
and this was a stroke

of genius, they put
a real woman (Surprise!)

on the seventh stair,
to stand for the pining ghost:

the girl Eurydice who
hiccupped all over

the American Indian Cemetery,
a cipher in isolation.

She revealed herself
to the scalene triangle the way

a town reveals itself
in the desert—generations

after breathing
under water.

(That's weather
for you.)

*

You, Eurydice,
crowd the sky

out of the river.
The cauliflower cloud

sinking into smoke, our mothers
with their red radios.

You hold a viewmaster
whose reel shows

the poster of
the MISSING GIRL,

and Harlequin
in his inflated hat.

Find him. Your brother
in the caves

has shapes
on his gown.

Yours is the tragedy
he cut his teeth on.

*

(Eurydice)

In the Indian Cemetery
they lifted the earth

and then they let us see.
I cannot unsee them

the mounds
way over the tiny traffic

the meager museum
with several grinding tools

at Cahokia.
No one had to lift me

to see the people
when they finished

all below us
bones with their vases,

bones with their children
bones curled into them

just where they were,
husks in the red grooves,

a fabulous building
all around us,

a wall, a screen
to show how they looked alive.

Someone buried them
again, decided it was wrong

to see,
but I saw them,

a sting in
my mouth,

the gentle moray
mouthing my heel.

*

Viewmaster says: pulpit, sanitorium, cinema, dining room, all
that the caves have been. And then Cahokia Mounds.

Note to self (Harlequin):

Dear Columbine,

>   *I was on a train. I was*
>   *looking out the window*
>   *at night and could only see myself.*
>   *And behind me in the window*
>   *I saw a man describe*
>   *how yesterday he saw*
>   *a hawk, and he mimicked*
>   *how the hawk hunkered down.*

>   *Harlequin*

V.

(Eurydice)

They take our picture
before we go down

into the cave,
in case one of us

goes missing.
A fan blows the group photos

of forty or so people
who might go missing

in the split second of the camera flash.
In the split second of seeing a 3

or an 8 in the camera flash, I turn
the number on its side, and it's

Oregon, 1938, the caves where
the Viewmaster was born.

Two cameras strapped
side-by-side

in plain sight
of Harold Graves.

Maybe the first
pictures on the circle

were the caves
of Oregon,

but then,
toys become gods.

Hand-held
gods.

(Child Chorus)

Viewmaster, we are feeling our
way across the photographs

on the reel. There is
the MISSING CHILD.

There is the sanctuary,
and the hospital, all cake walk

and dance contest.
There is the SNOWBALL

DINING ROOM that was really
a picture postcard photograph:

Viewmaster says: Columbine, Pierrot, Snack bar, Pierot's hands
writing a postcard in a gesture of immediate epistolarity,
Columbine reading the postcard he's slid over to her.

Dear Columbine:

> *We have just eaten our lunch*
> *in this dining room.*
> *I'm sitting at one of those*
> *tables writing this card.*
> *A week ago today we*
> *saw Carlsbad caverns.*
> *We will drive to Madison*
> *this p.m. to spend the Sabbath.*
> *So far all has gone per*
> *schedule. The Rambler is O.K.*
> *Best regards to all the boys.*
>
> *Pierrot*

And the picture on the postcard
is half the snowball dining room

and half a map of Eurydice's hometown,
Greater Sadorus, Illinois, in the shape of an arrowhead:

                    Lost Springs   **Lost Lodge**
       Lost Lake
            Lost Lincoln Drama   Lost Prairie   Lost River
                               Lost Cottage   Lost Town
                                          Lost Park

Lost Springs
            Lost Panther Creek   Lost New Salem   **Lost Grove**
            Lost Lake
            Lost Hart

                        Lost Tomb
                          Lost Gardens
                                        Lost Dell
                                        Lost Hill

               Lost Mount Lost Mount Lost Mount
                  Lost Brother Mine   **Lost Hidden Springs**
            Lost Lake
                              Lost River
                Lost Shoals   Lost Lake

Columbine laughs, slips the card into her purse.

VI.

(Child Chorus, some singing *We are Marching to Pretoria*)

Scrawl the map down, and *Greater Sadorus*
looks like snow.

Eurydice wears the cave as her disguise.
When she finally looks at Harlequin

mask and all, it's like looking in a mirror.
They are allies of revelation.

*

(Columbine): Soliloquy

Conversation meant more
than words on the page.
That's where I came from,
and talk without words
meant most: music, then,
the cabinet right by the door
with a door of its own
that opened on its side,
so why was the woman
dressed in *Whipped Cream*
leaning against the wall
over the refrigerator?

I mean, I stared up
at this woman of the
Herb Albert
and the Tijuana Brass album
Whipped Cream
all the time. She had
one hand to her mouth,
eating her dress, the mountain
she emerged from.

* (Columbine takes a breath.)

In our wedding portrait
we were two white owls
whose faces were hooked-nose masks.
We huddled on a limb
against a blue background.
The painter was from Texas. So was the sky.

(Eurydice to Harlequin): in the crawlspace

What book would I pretend
is blank and draw you?

An ink pen picture of you
over the *Concours de Moulins*,

you from the back
with your rabbit ears.

You holding a bee's nest
behind your back,

and a little man who holds
the circled drawing

of you by a string,
like a balloon.

You holding a star spearer
in front.

You rising above
the page number:

the eleven circled stars
in the book object.

Every plant has his
related star in the sky.

*

(Eurydice to Harlequin) A wrinkled MISSING CHILD poster
hugs the rock face.

You are seeing
the thing

you shall never
unsee: the outside

of the box,
the lunar rainbow

of the Aristotle
paraphrases,

and most especially
the burial ground,

the book object
covered with dust

and glass for Poe,
the spent meteor.

*

They took our picture
before we came down

into the cave,
in case one of us

went missing.
I went missing.

If only
you could read

the eggs
some *write*

for the dead.

*

Reading to Eurydice: (Harlequin): in the crawlspace:

    Columbine,

        To the one who said
        if only the moon
        would leave the night,
        here is his wish.
        I am learning German.
        I may meet K.
        in heaven.

        Harlequin

(Harlequin to Eurydice)

People have it all wrong
about resemblance.

I feel the pangs of likening
like needled sleep up my arms.

We sit in the wreck
of one or the other

of our fired-out
childhood houses,

and I hand you
a broken

coral necklace
that turns back into a doll

in your hands.
You say, this doll

is like you—
Its eyes are far away

and close up
at the same time.

(He draws the map of Eurydice's destination):

                         Lost Man Hole
                         Lost **Crawl Space Crawl Space Crawl Space Crawl Space**
                    Lost Mills   Lost Buffalo Lost Gleanings
                                                  Lost Mount
                              Lost Pike
                    Lost Springs
Lost Creek   Lost River
               Lost Bee Spring   Lost Lake
          Lost Ferry
                    Lost Onyx Cave
                    Lost Cave   Lost Horse Cave   Lost Springs
                         Lost Onyx Cave   Lost Sulphur Well
               Lost Hill
          Lost Springs   Lost Diamond Caverns
               Lost Forks Lost Soldier Divide
                         Lost Lake
                    Lost Run
               Lost Spring
Lost Land Lake
Lost Lake
                         Lost Lake
Lost Lake
               Lost Oak Lost Lake

*

After several miles,
Harlequin obeys the restraining order.

He rises up into a wet reflection
around the manhole. Sits,

(a heap of stones
erected as a memento

of an ascent.)
And Eurydice walks on.

VII.

(Eurydice to Columbine [finally], the swoop of her face like
snow)

I am the ribcage
showing through the roof.

I am the injury
in the hillside.

I am the woman
yelling and yelling at the river.

I am crying
the more you bleed.

I am the swarm
arriving with our comb.

I am a singer so good
my wolf shows through.

I am the prophet
you can't see floating.

I am the air that decides
when we move again.

I am a cave survivor,
muddy awkward as a new colt.

I am a jagged minstrel.
I am a fire on fire.

I am living
in all the circular languages.

I am the word that seduces you
back to the world.

(Columbine to Eurydice)

It wasn't my birthday
or anything, but there
were these snowy
dresses in the cave,
mammoth stalagmites
in plaster, like the **Whipped
Cream** dress on the old
Tijuana Brass album,
only these were wedding dresses,
and the plaster had dripped fingers up
around their trains,
at least one hand for each dress,
and somehow sunlight hit
a hand with its back to me,

and the plaster looked like skin
so real it scared me to death,
like someone coming
up out of the earth.

Two of the dresses
shouldered a red ladder.
Others had large
swollen books for wings,
bird cages dangerous
at the neck, or trees
arming their sleeves.
They're still here
somewhere in the caves.
Mary's feet at the cemetery
have the same hands
coming up around them,
but I thought of you first.   (Columbine exits.)

(Child Chorus)

The painter draws an arm
and draws an arm and draws
an arm, but she lets the hand
go out of the picture, so it has
a life of its own. She uses
a paragraph on the gold rush
to practice her cursive, the over
over, over of *miner*, and the
under, under, under of *rush*
in the manifest destiny, and she
draws the state of Illinois,
and marks the town of Sadorus,
and she draws the state

of Illinois from its straight top,
to its labial tip, and the tip
always embarrasses her
because the state has both
sexes, or maybe it's female,
and so she rushes the state
of Illinois, and it becomes very fat
by accident, and she has to draw it again,
this time, every time, with a hill
where the Indians are buried,
in the bowels of Illinois
where Cahokia is the name
of everything. She draws
the state of Illinois, and she
draws a horse's head, and she draws
a horse's head, and she draws a
horse's head and none
come out right, but at least the
horse looks a little like Sadorus,
and the state looks a little like it does.

(Eurydice to Pierrot)

My mother painted an ocean
by number,

before she ever
saw one.

She loved the flowers
whose smell was already fire.

The smell of my childhood
was burning flowers,

sun burning them
around the outhouse,

and tackle
wet in the evening,

and Styrofoam cup,
well water in the cup,

and sand so old its salt smell
comes from the soil

mixing up
from underneath.

*

Snow is elsewhere.
The black cilia of the music box

is elsewhere. My hands
are in the threads of his scarf.

I remember the hair
at the crown of his head.

The tiniest bit matted
from bed,

where the comb
didn't touch.

We were along the ocean
my mother painted by number.

A woman tapped her egg against
the inside of a moving train.

And whether the ants are conscious
and whether there are ants

in the forest, or whether the trees
are conscious, we do not know.

A woman tapped her egg against
the inside of a moving train,

and like the egg he brought me
in the dark,

she carried another world
in her face,

past a second story window open
over the ocean, no screen.

She could see through the moon
and our dream

did not look like a dream.
The dream had no train.

The whole world
stopped sounding like a world.

*

Pierrot the death mask
watches Eurydice remember

the photograph,
her eyes in the air.

He knows the moment
she thinks she sees herself

in the group picture.
She takes a breath.

He thinks she'd like to move
like a creature

who is only
head and wing.

Only the wind would be necessary.
She could count

the length of the day
with her pulse

the way Gallileo
navigated the small forms,

won all the prizes
at the health fair,

first prize for grip strength,
first prize for listing all the people.

he wanted to see in heaven.
As x approaches infinity.

As eight approaches infinity
by reclining.

(Eurydice exits.)

*

A crow flies behind
and below another crow

so Pierrot thinks at first
the second bird

is the first bird's shadow.
He closes the book

on a common house fly.
Like this Like this.

He shushes
the MISSING CHILD

who's been making faces at her portrait
all over town,

who holds the viewmaster
with every destination——

the smooth floor of the cave
in front of her tongue.

IV.

Imago Mundi

three war poems for Anselm Kiefer

I.

And in the painting
of the pool you've
added a wiry ship,
lead, ashes, and
a dress. Little planes
have landed on the ship,
shitting little fires; partly
they obscure the *lineline
linelinecrossthrough, linelinelinelinecrossthrough,*
of someone counting the laps
he swims. A little plane
comes out of each
orifice of the dress. The war
goes on. More little dresses
need to blow off the line,
and land on the painting's
little ship, but they don't.
There are no more dresses
over the pool or under
the aircraft carrier
in the post-war painting,
and they are miles from
a girl waking from a
sound sleep. Her feet
dangle. She is sitting
in for the bicycle
that sits in for the
angel, an artist's model

for a casualty, so tired
is she with her hair
hanging over her ears,
her striped coat behind
her on a hook. Her sleeves
rolled up over her shoulders,
she sits on the stretcher
balanced on treasure chest
and up-ended box. A sink
is in the room. The
porcelain gleams from the
corner. My bird sings to
the helicopters on
the television. Actresses
thin as ashes and pale as stone.
This ship on the pool wall,
the same. Ashes. Stone.
When my birds sings,
it's a needle in the air.
In the distance, the artist's model
for a wounded angel
with her hair hanging
over her ears. She'll give
us the time of day in heaven.

II.

In the morning, jack-in-the-box music
from an upstairs apartment. It's strung along
so the clown never arrives, *linelineline
crossthrough, linelinelinelinecrossthrough,* origin of
millennium approximate, carbon of isotope,
the high caves spring-fed behind the leaving
limestone. The red hummingbird water

is sun-bleached clear on the porch rail. Perhaps
peaceful more, yes, peaceful more.
Wall of traces lasts. Glass of shards
lasts. Say to the Book's leaden heavens
the Beneath that lies over everything.
This from stones, this from roots,
this from the molecule's chill fleet
and loam cataracting and claws that have mechanized,
the building glass shining past, and night
which we have moved along the road.

Discovered were the old years:
the vast *how* that decays the measure,
needleneedleneedleneedle   needleneedleneedleneedle,
the structure natural in the cracks
and lines flowing wonderfully,
the secret wasp nest that fanned out
and filled up a murdered child's skull (inside her
secret kiln grave) with tiny rooms,
(dark in there) (dizzying, the comparison),
the little leaden dresses strewn
on their burned black hangers
like tombstones, only they aren't.
They are creation secrets, leaden dresses
the size of a thumb, and some
the size of a body, blowing up
around the door of the abandoned
silk factory, and spinning in the coliseum
like a little flesh chime in an age
whose bestiary grows and grows.
Say to the factory large of gate:
Grass will grow over our cities.

III.

Someone wrote over the old lines
with new ones. *linelinelinelinecrossthrough 12.8*
linelinelinelinecrossthrough 12:34 linelinelinelinecrossthrough lineline

linelinecrossthrough

73:59 linelinelinelinecrossthrough 28.7 linelinelinelinecrossthrough

Fr. 30.7 linelinelinecrossthrough

linelinelinelinecrossthrough Di 3.8 linelinelinelinecrossthrough

12 12

Only they upturn and crowd, imperfect as fingers imperfect as fingers,
and they swirl and join in the pool water.
The lightning strike of pool's cracked cement
hits them. The light from the water
scribbles over the storm cloud colors.
One line for each lap, and sometimes
a time in the forest on the old pool wall.

The lines waver in the group photographs,
the lines come closer and closer until
there's only texture of swimming pool,
the grains of charcoal. The groups of lines
float above the old pool upturned
almost in flight, a bird made of charcoal laps.
I should have been a falconer
above this pool (somewhere in Germany).

Where I have seen this language before.
So turned, so corroded, the needles
threading the yellow satin
look like nails on their ends, lines and lines
and black lines of them, three hundred
sources of anticipation removed
from the lunatic who mistook the needles
for the drug, and now they are saved
like a sewing kit, quiet grotesque
needleneedleneedleneedle   needleneedleneedleneedle,
needleneedleneedleneedle,
and so on on the shining fabric,
but these are in a line, these are long
and short and in lines, not the sweep upward
of the bird of the pool wall.

Something about an old swimming pool
haunted by counting: Here's my time today.
Here is my time yesterday, and the day before.
Grotto with the clearest picture of time, no
exaggeration, if you put your hand up
to the wall, you'll see the stone is still
warm——though the cave is mostly dark.

I am a falconer coaxing
these lines together into a bird
toward my leather wrist. Removing little
fringed hoods for the rest of the day.
I keep hearing myself saying,
for as long as I am a falconer,
Lines, keep heaping beauty on me.

Notes

Imago mundi was the title of one of the first books on geography ever written. Pierre d'Ailly wrote *Imago mundi* in 1410, and it became Christopher Columbus' favorite book. He heavily annotated his own copy.

In "Pam at the Rock of Forgetting," the Greek word for "ribbon" is *lemniscate*, which is the technical term for the infinity symbol, called "a scab of symbols" by Thomas Hobbes (Thank you, David Foster Wallace, for the tidbit and for *Everything and More*, which furthered my consideration of the symbol).

"Three of Mary" remembers Mary the mother of Jesus, Marie Laveau, and Delphine Lalaverie: the Mother of God, the voodoo priestess, and the serial killer. The poem also remembers Mary Magdalene. "Mary" is also another name for "girl" or "woman." "Mary" is derived from the Aramaic word for "rebellion."

Other Titles From
ELIXIR PRESS

The Jewish Fake Book
Sima Rabinowitz
1-932418-07-5 • $13
Recital
Samn Stockwell
1-932418-08-3 • $13
Assignation at Vanishing Point
Jane Satterfield
0-9709342-9-7 • $13
Running the Voodoo Down
Jim McGarrah
0-9709342-8-9 • $13
Drag
Duriel E. Harris
1-932418-00-8 • $14
Flow Blue
Sarah Kennedy
0-9709342-5-4 • $13
Monster Zero
Jay Snodgrass
0-9709342-6-2 • $13
Circassian Girl
Michelle Mitchell-Foust
0-9709342-2-X • $13
Distance From Birth
Tracy Philpot
0-9709342-1-1 • $13

Original White Animals
Tracy Philpot
1-932418-13-X

How Things Break
Kerala Goodkin
1-932418-14-8

Limited Edition Chapbooks
Rapture
Sarah Kennedy
Poetry
1-932418-05-9 • $7
X-Testaments
Karen Zealand
Poetry
1-932418-02-4 • $7
Juju
Judy Moffett
Fiction
1-932418-01-6 • $11
Grass
Sean Aden Lovelace
Fiction
1-932418-04-0 • $8